# STUDENT WORKBOOK for
# THE JOURNEY THROUGH THE LIFE SPAN:
## AN OBSERVATION GUIDE FOR DEVELOPMENT

to accompany

Kathleen Stassen Berger
*The Developing Person Through the Life Span*

D1432166

## S. Stavros Valenti
Hofstra University

WORTH PUBLISHERS

Student Workbook
for
**THE JOURNEYTHROUGH THE LIFE SPAN:**
**AN OBSERVATION GUIDE FOR DEVELOPMENT**
A supplement to Kathleen Stassen Berger,
*The Developing Person Through the Life Span*

ISBN: 0-7167-5207-7  (EAN:  9780716752073)


9th printing 2007


Printed in the United States of America

Worth Publishers
41 Madison Avenue
New York, NY 10010
www.worthpublishers.com

# Contents

# Introduction:
# The Importance of Observation

The hero of Arthur Conan Doyle's popular detective novels, Sherlock Holmes, continually amazed his friend Dr. Watson with his powers of observation. On one occasion he correctly deduced that Watson had been caught in the rain a day or so ago, and that he has a very clumsy housekeeper. When asked to explain his reasoning, Holmes pointed out scrape marks on Watson's upper boot leather, the result of careless removal of mud. Commenting on Holmes's process of deduction, Watson remarked: "When I hear you give your reasons, the thing always appears to me to be so ridiculously simple that I could easily do it myself, though at each successive instance of your reasoning I am baffled, until you explain your process. And yet I believe that my eyes are as good as yours." "Quite so," Sherlock Holmes answered. "You see, but you do not observe" (Doyle, 1891).

Observing is not just seeing: It is a way of watching and interacting that reveals more of the subject's hidden qualities and talents. All of the sciences, including psychology, use specific observation methods to gather facts and support theories. This workbook, along with your textbook and video, *The Journey Through the Life Span*, is designed to help you become a better observer of people.

It has been my experience that the best observers—experienced parents, skilled teachers, and diligent students of development—notice more when they observe people, and because they do, their work is more enjoyable. Four-month-old infants are not very good at handling objects, but watch closely and you will see them "grasping" with their eyes. An 18-month-old infant who cries and cries when his mother leaves the room is most likely a very secure and happy toddler—which you could deduce if you watched closely what he does when his mother returns. The typical two-year-old is learning a new word every two hours on average, and three-year-olds make surprisingly few grammatical errors, if you listen word for word. Adolescents may seem to take senseless risks, but if you speak with them you may discover how risk creates a sense of responsibility. Older adults who have found the right balance of love and work surround us. Careful observation and listening allow you to share the secret of their success.

Sometimes people do things you don't expect, and other times they don't do things you want them to do. The more you know about humans of all ages, and the more you observe them, the less likely you will misinterpret their behavior. And if you truly understand what you see, your work with children and adults will be more effective. A similar conclusion was reached by the painter and teacher Thomas Eakins, who required every student to study anatomy in the firm conviction that "knowing all that will enable him to observe more closely, and the closer his observation is the better his drawing will be" (Brownell, 1879). The work of the artist and scientist is made stronger by skilled observation. The same will be true of your work.

Toward this end, some of the observation exercises in this workbook are designed to highlight the behaviors you will read about in the text, just as the text will prepare you to notice more in the video *The Journey Through the Life Span*. Outside of the classroom you will see hundreds of examples of these behaviors in homes, playgrounds, classrooms, parks, and workplaces—wherever children and adults are found. Other exercises are based on commonly used research techniques in the study of children and adolescents, such as diary descriptions, anecdotal records, event sampling, time sampling, behavior rating, and interviews.

Some of these observation techniques may prove useful later in your academic or professional career. If your professional goal is teaching, you will need to observe children's reasoning, problem solving, and interactions with other children every day in order to form a fuller picture of their intellectual and emotional growth, and to see areas where you can assist. Some students of human development eventually work in human services, as psychologists, counselors, and social workers. In these settings, you will need to observe behaviors, thoughts, and feelings of clients of all ages. Even in non-scientific fields, such as business or government, observation can help you understand and interact more effectively with co-workers. Many of the observational techniques illustrated here are general and can be used by professionals in any setting where the goal is to better understand human behavior.

I have collected these assignments to help you observe more closely, which will help you understand better the marvelous story of human development. But more importantly, I want you to see and be amazed by children and adults across the life span.

S. Stavros Valenti
Hofstra University

# Birth

## A. NARRATED VIDEO ASSIGNMENT

*Key terms*

Apgar Scale
preterm infant
vernix caseosa

*Rating the newborn*

1. Immediately after birth, the infant's skin is covered with a white cheese-like substance, called the
_____ _____, which protects the baby against infection.

2. The _____ scale is used to assess the newborn's condition at one minute and again at five minutes.
It rates five newborn characteristics: _____, _____, _____, _____, and _____ .

*Premature babies*

3. A _____ infant is any baby born before the 37th week after conception.

4. The risk of a premature birth can be increased because of drugs such as _____ or _____.

5. Complications like _____ _____ and _____ _____ can also elevate the risk of a
premature birth.

6. Some studies indicate that infants born prematurely may perform lower on _____ tests later in life,
but this is not always the case.

*Thought questions*

7. What do you think would be the best national strategy for coping with the problem of premature infant
births?

8. Emotional bonding between caretakers and infants begins at birth, but the amount of contact may be limited by the medical needs of a preterm infant. What can hospitals do to promote early bonding between parents and their preterm infants?

## B. OBSERVATION MODULE ASSIGNMENT

1. Premature infants (4:15)

a. Provide your best estimate of Taylor's age in weeks since conception. Pay close attention to his weight and size, the level of medical attention he is receiving, and any other contextual factors that are relevant to his medical condition.

b. Identify all of the ways this preterm infant is being assisted with extra medical attention.

c. What is the reason for the tape over the preterm infant's nose?

d. Why is there a "hat" on this preterm infant?

e. What can the mother or father do to assist the development of a preterm infant, such as Taylor, who needs to remain in the hospital during the first weeks of life?

## C. FIELD ASSIGNMENT

Interview with a pregnant mother

Pregnancy is one of the most novel and remarkable events a woman will experience. Many women are happy to speak with others about their own experience with pregnancy, and my students have always enjoyed speaking with an expectant parent.

For this assignment you will interview a woman who is pregnant, and then write a summary of your observations with reference to (a) her thoughts about the experience of pregnancy, and (b) her expectations for her child and for herself—that is, what she expects her child to be like and what she expects from herself as a future parent.

Take a look at the material in your book on prenatal development and birth before you begin your interview, to get some sense of the type of questions you will want to ask. Next, find a woman who is pregnant and willing to speak with you for 5 to 10 minutes about her experience. Perhaps you know a friend or family member who is expecting a child, or who can recommend someone who would speak with you in person or over the phone.

Ask any questions of your own in this interview. To get things started, here are a few sample questions; use only those you feel comfortable asking:

- What trimester of pregnancy do you think is or will be the easiest for you?
- How often have you been visiting a medical professional during the pregnancy?
- How do you feel about how your body is changing during pregnancy?
- How do you feel, in general, about having a baby?
- How do other members of your family feel about having a baby?
- Do you know if your child is a boy or a girl? If not, would you prefer a girl or a boy?
- Are you making any changes in your home to prepare for the arrival of your child?
- Do you have other children? If so, are they looking forward to the arrival of the new baby?
- Have you changed your diet in any ways? Do you have "cravings"?
- If this is not your first baby, has this pregnancy been easier or more difficult than the last?
- Have you named your baby yet? If so, what will his or her name be? How did you select his or her name?
- What do you think your baby will be like?
- What do you think you will be like as a parent?
- What do you think is the most important task of a parent?
- Do you think you will change in some significant ways after the arrival of this baby?
- Is there anything you are doing to prepare yourself for the arrival of this baby?
- Is there anything you would like to tell me about your experiences or thoughts about being a parent?

Take good notes. If possible, tape record the interview. Type the questions and answers in a page or so as soon as you are able, and then write a summary paragraph as suggested above (i.e., expectations about the baby and about the self).

# Early Infancy

## A. NARRATED VIDEO ASSIGNMENT

*Key terms*

babinski reflex
breathing reflex
endogenous smile
exogenous smile
eyeblink reflex
grasping reflex
hunger cry
moro reflex

pain cry
rooting reflex
sleeping patterns
social smile
stepping reflex
sucking reflex
swallowing reflex

*Newborn reflexes*

1. The _____ reflex, turning the head and opening the mouth, occurs when the side of a newborn's cheek is stimulated.

2. The _____ reflex occurs whenever an object, like a nipple or a finger, is placed in the newborn's mouth.

3. Liquids in the mouth lead automatically to the _____ reflex.

4. A precursor to walking is the _____ reflex.

5. Stimulating the sole of the newborn's foot causes the toes to fan out and curl—the _____ reflex.

6. The _____ reflex can be strong enough to support the infant's weight.

7. When startled or dropped, the newborn may throw the arms outward and then inward. This is known as the _____ reflex.

8. The sense of _____ is one of the least developed at birth, although one-month-old Lily is able to distinguish between sweet and sour.

*Sleeping*

9. Infants need about _____ hours of sleep each day.

10. Compared to North American families, Dutch families place _____ emphasis on the importance of sleep for healthy development.

*Smiling*

11. Before the first month, the _____ smile is observed in infants. It seems to be caused more by internal than by external stimulation.

12. An indiscriminate facial expression that occurs between the first and third month is the _____ smile.

13. Genuine _____ smiles occur around the third month in response to the facial expressions of other persons.

*Crying*

14. The _____ cry is high-pitched and fast.

15. The _____ cry is slower and lower in pitch.

*Thought questions*

16. Human babies are born in a less developed state compared to the infants of our closest evolutionary relatives, the apes. Do you think that the more helpless state of human infants has any adaptive advantages for our uniquely human way of life?

17. What is the adaptive significance of the human smile? In other words, how does the human smile fit the human way of life?

18. Some babies are born without sight, and therefore they will never see another person smile. How do you think this could change the course of their social and emotional development? How could this change the style of parenting?

## B. OBSERVATION MODULE ASSIGNMENTS

1. Newborn reflexes (3:15)

a. Estimate the age of this infant.  Is the infant a boy or a girl?  How can you tell?

b. Identify as many reflexes as you can. Give the name of the reflex as well as a brief description of it as seen on the video module.

c. At one point the infant begins to cry.  What, if anything, appears to be the reason for this crying?

d. Make note of any other observations you think may be relevant.

2. Young infant in various states of arousal (5:35)

a. While you watch this video module, list and briefly describe Julia's various states of arousal.

b. Is their any evidence that Julia recognizes her mother?

c. Estimate Julia's age.  What is it about the behavior of this infant that affected your age estimate?

## C. FIELD ASSIGNMENT

*Infant reflexes*

Most observers are surprised to see firsthand the early reflexes of a very young infant. A rooting reflex—turning the head in the direction of stimulation on the cheek—is somewhat sluggish, and not quick in the way we imagine a "knee-jerk" reflex to be. All the same, the reflexes are organized bouts of behavior, and they appear without being taught within the first minutes of life.

If you have access to an infant between one and three months of age, try to observe the following reflexes. Use your textbook as a guide for how to elicit each reflex, and write a brief description of the reaction you observe. It is also a good idea to have the principal caregiver present and to explain what you are going to do before you attempt to elicit each reflex. If the caregiver cannot be present, explicitly ask for permission, and explain each of the reflexes you wish to demonstrate.

Babinski _____

_____

_____

Breathing[1] _____

_____

_____

Crawling _____

_____

_____

Eyeblink[2] _____

_____

_____

Grasping _____

_____

_____

Moro[3] _____

_____

_____

Rooting _____

_____

_____

Stepping _____

_____

_____

Sucking _____

_____

_____

*Notes*:

[1]This may seem like a trivial reflex, but take a closer look. What is the rate of breathing? Are there any pauses, such as when the infant notices a new object in the visual field or hears an unexpected sound?

[2]Of course, you don't want to put anything in the infant's eye. Try moving an object toward the baby's face (i.e., looming) or blowing a very gentle puff of air from 12 inches away.

[3]I strongly suggest that you describe the moro reflex to the caregiver and let them try to elicit it, because it requires the sudden removal of support from the head. They have probably noticed this response when moving the baby from place to place. Sometimes a loud and unexpected sound will also elicit this reflex.

# Infants and Toddlers

## A. NARRATED VIDEO ASSIGNMENT

*Key terms*

A-not-B error
affordances
babbling
dendrites
grammatical function words
habituation
holophrase
imitation
infant body proportions
insecure attachment
Jean Piaget
language
locomotor development
manual development
motherese (child-directed speech)
myelination

object constancy
object permanence
perception
perceptual constancy
pincer grasp
secure attachment
self-awareness
sensorimotor development
separation anxiety
social referencing
stranger anxiety
synchrony
telegraphic speech
temperament (easy, slow to warm up, difficult)
universal grammar

*Growing quickly*

1. The average newborn weighs less than a _____ of milk and is about _____ inches long.

2. Over the first year, infants grow approximately _____ inch a month.

3. The newborn's head is about _____ percent of her body length; in adults, the head is only about 13 percent of the body length.

4. During the first year, the _____ —thin branch-like structures though which neurons communicate—become more dense.

5. Transmission of neural signals is accelerated as a consequence of _____ of the neurons.

*Motor development*

6. Before an infant can crawl and walk, she needs to be able to hold up her _____.

7. At about five or six months of age, and infant can sit up without _____ .

8. By about _____ months, most infants are accomplished crawlers.

9.  Walking is usually seen at about _____ months.

10.  Many infants can kick a ball at around _____ months of age.

11.  The _____ grasp—a precise grip using the finger and thumb—is well established by _____ months.

*Perceiving objects, surfaces, and people*

12.  Interaction opportunities provided by the environment are called _____ .

13.  Every object can have multiple _____ .

14.  A crawling infant can learn how to safely move down a steep slope, as did the baby in studies by researcher Karen Adolph.  When the same baby later learns to _____, she will have to learn all over again about which slopes are safe and which are not.

15.  Perceptual _____ refers to the fact that people perceive a constant object even though the visual image may get larger or smaller at varying distances from the object.

*Object permanence and memory*

16.  _____ occurs when an infant stops attending to an object or event with repeated exposure.

17.  Infants understand object _____ when they search for objects that are hidden from view.

18.  The _____ - _____ - _____ error occurs when an infant looks for an object where he last found it, even thought the object was moved to a new place in clear view of the infant.

19.  Stranger wariness emerges between 9 and 12 months of age, and is one indication that the infant's _____ capacity is increasing.

*Piaget's stages of sensorimotor development*

20.  During the second stage of sensorimotor development—between one and four months—infants begin to _____ their reflexes to new objects, according to Jean Piaget.

21.  In the fourth stage of sensorimotor development—between 8 and 12 months—infants show clear evidence of _____ events and goal-oriented behavior.

22.  By the sixth stage of sensorimotor development, infants are beginning to solve problems in their _____ and require less trial and error.

*Language development*

23. Infants have a _____ capacity to acquire words and grammar.

24. The repetition of syllables a baby produces between 6 and 10 months of age is called _____ . These sounds are the building blocks of true speech.

25. Infants begin to understand true words around _____ months.

26. By 18 months of age, most infants are learning about _____ words a day.

27. _____ _____ refers to speech that contains only the most important words, such as "Mommy milk!"

*Emotional development and social interaction*

28. _____ _____ describes the baby's signs of uneasiness around strangers in the second half of the first year.

29. Babies often look for their parents' reactions when they themselves are faced with a novel situation. This search for cues from the caregivers is called _____ _____ .

30. The fear of being separated from a primary caregiver is called _____ _____ .

31. The special bond that emerges between caregivers and babies is called _____ .

32. _____ _____ is said to exist when one-year-old infants become distressed when separated from their caregiver, but later are easily soothed by the caregiver when she or he returns.

33. The early personality of infants—their typical style of coping with new people and environmental demands—is called _____ .

34. Forty percent of babies are classified as_____ . These are cheerful babies who love to play, adapt easily, and eat and sleep at regular times.

35. Fifteen percent of babies are _____ _____ _____ _____ . That is, they are finicky eaters, often don't sleep well, and respond poorly to new people or situations.

*Thought questions*

36. In what ways do changes in the postural and locomotor skills of infants affect their perceptual experiences?

37. According to Jean Piaget, mental representations and symbolic capacity grow out of basic reflex actions. Simply stated, reflexes such as sucking grow into remembering and planning. Is there any one stage of sensorimotor development that seems pivotal in the transition from reflexive to thoughtful behavior in infancy?

38. What kinds of biological and social factors allow the toddler to acquire language so rapidly?

39. Present an argument for why a difficult temperament, under some circumstances, may be an optimal temperament.

## B. OBSERVATION MODULE ASSIGNMENTS

1. Two infants lying down (0:50)

a. Can you tell which of Piaget's sensorimotor stages best describes these two infants, Boris and Skye? Justify your answer.

b. Is anything about these infants' behavior relevant to the development of speech?

c. Is there any evidence of accommodation in their behavior?

d. Approximately what are the ages of these infants? What features of behavior, size, or shape support your age estimate?

2.  Toddlers in a playroom (5:00)

a.  Describe all of the forms of locomotor behavior observed among these toddlers.  Does each toddler have a preferred method of locomotion, or does it depend upon the context?

b.  Briefly describe the play of each child (Rylen in blue, Maya in pink, Lilith with red hair in the yellow dress, and Samantha with blond hair in the yellow shirt) using your textbook's descriptions of play types as a guide.

c.  Is there any evidence of symbolic play in their activities?

d.  Is their play in any sense "social"?

e.  Estimate the ages of each of these toddlers. What evidence is there for your estimates?

3.  Toddler in a highchair (4:20)

a.  Listen closely to the language used by Emma.  How would you describe her level of speech development?

b.  What would you guess is the number of words she can speak?  What can you say about her level of comprehension of language?

c.  Are her parents doing anything in particular to assist her language development?  Identify all of the ways they are helping Emma to develop language.

d.  Look closely as Emma manipulates the small objects (grapes) on her highchair tray.  How would you describe her skills of fine motor control?

e.  From all that you have seen and heard, what is your best estimate of Emma's age?

## C. FIELD ASSIGNMENTS

1. Observing mealtimes:  The socialization of action

Actions, like eating with a fork, are more than simple responses to stimuli. They are patterns of living that are shaped by both the child and the environment. This two-sided process of shaping actions is often called social co-construction (e.g., Valsiner, 1988).

You may not be thinking about a two-sided process when watching a toddler at mealtime; it often looks as if the toddler is calling all the shots. A two-year-old may pick up foods, drop them, refuse foods offered to her, squish foods on the plate, and in general make a mess. But watch closely, and you will see a two-sided process as the caregiver tries to ease the toddler toward socially accepted means of eating (e.g., not smearing, not spilling, not playing with foods, using a spoon for some foods and a fork for other foods, etc.).

For this assignment, take careful notes during at least 10 minutes of a mealtime for a toddler between the ages of two and three. Keep a running record of everything the child and the caregiver do during feeding. Describe each partner's actions on alternating lines as in the following example:

ANDY, two years one month, with his father (C = child, P = parent)

- C: (Picks up cereal flakes and puts a few in mouth. Then drops some on the floor.)
- P: "No no NO" (laughs and eats a few himself). "Like this."
- C: (Holds up some cereal flakes, opens mouth, giggles, and drops them on the tray.)
- P: "Oh, you're something!" (eats a few flakes).

When you are finished, read over your notes and write a paragraph that describes the two-sided process of controlling (regulating) mealtime activities. What unsocialized and socialized eating actions did the child show? Did the child imitate or model the parent? Did the parent imitate the child? Did the child ever tease the parent? How did the parent attempt to reward the child for appropriate mealtime behaviors?

In class, you can compare your notes on mealtime actions with someone who observed a child of the same age and with a second person that observed a child of a different age (say, six months older or younger).

2. Language skills of a three-year-old

Few abilities change as dramatically as does that of language between a child's first and third birthday. Toddlers learn on average a new word every two hours and keep up this rate of learning until adolescence. If you listen carefully to three-year-olds, many of their statements are somewhat simple yet perfectly grammatical. These observations have lead Dr. Steven Pinker of MIT to refer to three-year-olds as "grammatical geniuses," because they accomplish these feats of learning without explicit instruction.

The best way to see the language skills of three-year-olds is to transcribe everything they say and then take a good look at it. For this exercise you will need a three-year-old (with the parent's consent, of course), a tape recorder, and a safe place to play and talk. Any tape recorder will do, and most have built-in microphones. Many of the larger "boom-boxes" can record tapes just as well. Since you will be recording sound, it will be better to find an indoor setting or a relatively quiet outdoor location. A particularly good place, I think, is a play kitchen, where you and the child can act out a familiar routine such as "mealtime at home" or "going to McDonalds."

Now, engage the toddler in play, encourage him or her to talk, and ask any questions that seem appropriate, such as "What shall we do next?" or "What's that?"

Later on, transcribe your tape recording word for word. Note the speaker in the left margin (C = Child, O = Observer), and start each speaker's turn on a new line.

When you are finished with your transcripts, put an asterisk (*) to the left of any child statement that is not grammatically correct. You will be surprised to see that much of what they say is simple but correct, and most of the errors are omissions of the little "function words," such as *am* or contractions of *to be*, and not errors of word order.

As you read over the transcript, look for the following features of language described in your text and write out the word or phrase from your transcripts that illustrates each feature. The grammatical morphemes are arranged in the order in which they are typically acquired.

Overextension    _____

Underextension    _____

Holophrase    _____

Two-word utterance    _____

Three-word utterance    _____

Tag question    _____

Grammatical morphemes

    present progressive    _____

    *in*    _____

    *on*    _____

    plural    _____

    past irregular    _____

    possessive inflection    _____

    *to be* not contracted    _____

    article    _____

    past regular    _____

    third-person regular    _____

    third-person irregular    _____

    uncontractable progressive

      auxiliary    _____

    contractions of

      *to be*    _____

    contractable  progressive

      auxiliary    _____

(Adapted from Cole & Cole, 1996, p. 310.)

# Early Childhood

## A. NARRATED VIDEO ASSIGNMENT

*Key terms*

authoritative parenting
autocratic parenting
categorization
cognitive development
concrete operations
conservation tasks
egocentrism
fast mapping
fine-motor skills
gender differences
grammatical patterns
gross-motor skills
growth spurt
guided participation
Jean Piaget

Lev Vygotsky
mastery play
memory
number
overgeneralization
overregularization
parallel play
permissive parenting
rehearsal
scripts
self-esteem
sensorimotor play
sociodramatic play
zone of proximal development

*Motor development*

1. During the growth spurt of early childhood, the bones of the arms and legs will _____, contributing to a slimmer, adult-like appearance.

2. _____ is a favorite activity of many children, once they develop a strong upper body and a tight grip.

3. It takes more time for _____ - _____ skills to develop compared to gross-motor skills.

*Cognitive development*

4. Even toddlers know that numbers have a _____ order.

5. Older children use rehearsal and categorization as aids to memory. Younger children, however, fail to use many of these basic memory _____ .

6. Adults often ask young children about familiar or repeated activities, such as "going to McDonalds." Knowledge about these familiar activities is called a mental _____ .

7. The tendency of children to understand the world and events from their own point of view is called _____, and it can be seen in the way children talk to one another and in the way they answer questions.

8. Piaget used the _____ task to test whether children had reached the concrete operational stage of thought.

9. Lev Vygotsky emphasized the importance of guided _____ with adults as the way children learn new skills. These interactions with adults create a "zone of _____ development" in which higher psychological functions are formed.

*Language development*

10. Language is first used to control others, but a preschooler can also talk to _____, using speech to steer her own actions.

11. At _____ years of age, children speak in only one- or two-word sentences.

12. By age _____, a preschooler has become a "grammatical genius" and uses most of the grammatical structures of adults.

13. Even before a child completely understands a word, they put it into a mental category, a process called _____ _____ .

14. When a child says "goed" instead of "went" we know that she is learning the _____ of grammar.

*Styles of parenting*

15. In _____ parenting, the caregivers are the experts in the household, and they work with their children to guide their behavior, but are not overly controlling.

16. In contrast, _____ parents are very controlling. This may lead to children who are overly fearful or who are rebellious.

17. The _____ - _____ style of parenting is also known as permissive parenting. Under this style, children typically are less competent and self-controlled compared to their peers.

*Play*

18. When children toy with their food or smell flowers, they're engaging in _____ play, which involves the pleasure of using the senses.

19. Most of the repetitive activity you see at a playground is probably _____ play, where children practice a specific skill like jumping or throwing.

20. Activities that involve acting out and role playing comprise _____ play.

21. Two- and three-year-olds sometimes play side by side but not really with each other. This is called _____ play.

22. As children grow older, play begins to show average differences according to gender. While not absolutely different, boys tend to gravitate toward larger groups and games with stricter rules, whereas girls more often will play together in smaller groups in games that require _____ and _____ .

*Thought questions*

23. In your opinion, what is the most critical trait of preschoolers that makes it difficult for them to master new skills? Explain your answer.

24. Reflecting on your own upbringing, what style of parenting did you experience? What parental behaviors support your choice?

25. Is there any connection between the kinds of mental activity seen in sociodramatic play, on the one hand, and logical thought, on the other?

## B. OBSERVATION MODULE ASSIGNMENTS

1. Preschool children playing with toy train tracks (1:10)

a. Make a transcript of every statement made by these three children. How would you describe their levels of speech development?

b. To what extent can their play activities be described as "social"?

c. Estimate the range of ages for these three children. What features of behavior or appearance led to your estimate?

2. Boys and girls with dolls, play food, and reading (5:50)

a. Describe the setting and content of the interaction among the four children in the kitchen play area.

b. Compare the same-gender interactions with the cross-gender interactions for these children in the kitchen play area.

c. Carefully watch the boy and girl in the reading area. At one point the boy will push the girl. How would you explain this behavior?

d. Estimate the age range of the children seen in this video module. What features of behavior or appearance influenced your estimate?

3. Young children in playground (1:30)

a. Describe the setting and content of the interaction on this playground. Pay particular attention at the start of the video module to the boy on the ground and the girl with the small red plastic scooper.

b. What do you think provoked this conflict between the boy and the girl?

c. If possible, watch this scene again, this time attending to the two other children—the small boy in the blue shorts and the girl in the green swimsuit. Describe and explain their behavior as best as you can.

d. What do these interactions say about the role of observational learning in young children's social development?

e. Estimate the ages of these four children (boy in conflict, girl in conflict, boy in blue shorts, girl in green swimsuit). What features of behavior, context, or physical appearance influenced your estimates?

4. Two young boys playing Musketeers with swords (1:35)

a. Describe the setting and content of this interaction between the two boys, Tom (dark shirt) and Jonah (red shirt) in the backyard.

b. How would you describe the particular form of play seen in this interaction?

c. Describe how the play activity is negotiated, if at all, by these two boys and their parents. How does the play move from one type of activity to the next? Is there any discussion? Does one child determine the play topic more so than the other?

d. From what you have observed, what is your best estimate of the ages of Tom and Jonah?

## C. FIELD ASSIGNMENTS

1. Piagetian clinical interview

Jean Piaget's early research on the speech of young children used an interview method—rather than a rigidly controlled experimental procedure—to assess the quality of the young child's thinking. The point was not to see if the child could answer correctly, but rather to see the process of the child's thought. Using this method Piaget concluded that young children say many things they never heard before. Therefore, they must be actively constructing their own understanding of reality.

For this brief assignment, you will be asking a three- or four-year-old child two simple questions: (a) Where does the sun go at night? and (b) Where do dreams come from?

Audiotape your interview, and after each question, see if you can encourage the child to elaborate on their answer. It is best to do this with open-ended questions, such as "And then what happens?" Avoid closed-ended questions that prompt the child for a yes or no answer, such as "Does the sun go home?"

After your interview, transcribe your questions and the child's answers word for word. Then, write a brief paragraph summarizing your observations with reference to Piaget's descriptions of preoperational thinking.

2.  Identifying a dominant child in a playgroup

While it may not be apparent upon casual inspection, playgroups of three- and four-year-old children often show a social ordering, known as a dominance hierarchy. If you closely watch any two children, one of them is more likely than the other to initiate aggressive acts (e.g., tussles over possessions or verbal threats) and the other is more likely to withdraw (e.g., cry, flinch, or seek an adult). Across a group of three or four children, therefore, one of them is likely to be dominant over all of the others. The dominant child is not always threatening other children; rather, this child usually gets his or her way, and the other children usually do not act aggressively toward the dominant child (Strayer, 1991).

One way to observe and record the activities of a playgroup over time, and to identify a dominant child, is to make a specimen description—a record of behavior over time to yield a sample (specimen) of the phenomenon in question. Slee (1987) presents a number of guidelines for making specimen descriptions, some of which are briefly described here:

• Describe the scene as accurately as possible.
• Describe what the child does, and how the child does it (e.g., He ran quickly in circles five times and said "I'm a cowboy!").
• When you write your interpretations of behavior, put them in brackets (e.g., [He is imitating what he saw in the picture book a few minutes ago]).
• Describe other people's reaction to the child's behavior.
• Use a wristwatch or a stopwatch, and put your observations in order.
• When you are finished recording your observations, mark the beginning of each behavior episode—"a unit of behavior that describes a particular situation and some ongoing behavior in that setting" (Slee, 1987, p. 37).

After making your specimen description, write a brief paragraph identifying the dominant child and explaining your choice of this particular child.

### Specimen Description of Preschool Play Group

Today's date: _____
Children's names and ages: _____

Observation start time: _____
Observation stop time: _____

Begin (Minute 0)

_____
_____
_____
_____
_____
_____

Minute 5

_____
_____
_____
_____
_____
_____

Minute 10

_____
_____
_____
_____
_____
_____

Minute 15

_____
_____
_____
_____
_____
_____

Minute 20

_____
_____
_____
_____
_____
_____

Minute 25

_____
_____
_____
_____
_____
_____

Minute 30

_____
_____
_____
_____
_____
_____

# Middle Childhood

## A. NARRATED VIDEO ASSIGNMENT

*Key terms*

bully
cognitive strategies
concrete operational thought
conservation tasks
empathy
friendship
gender segregation
metacognition

moral values
peer groups
physical aggression
prosocial behavior
relational aggression
selective attention
social rules
sympathy

*Physical development*

1. During the school years, children's physical development levels off. Still, they are gaining about _____ pounds and growing _____ inches every year.

2. Boys have greater _____ mass compared to girls. This gives them an advantage in skills that require greater power, force, and upper-body strength.

3. Girls have much greater _____ and _____ than boys, yielding better dexterity and poise.

*Language*

4. By the fifth grade (age 10) children's vocabulary is typically around _____ words.

5. School-age children have a solid understanding of _____ , the patterns of arrangement and relations among words in speech.

*Attention and thinking*

6. _____ _____ is the ability to screen out distractions and focus on a given task.

7. School children have a better understanding of their own thought processes. In other words, they can think about thinking. This is known as _____ .

8. Children in different societies learn culture-specific strategies for thinking and problemsolving. For example, Dr. Geoffrey Saxe has studied the Oksapmin children of Papua New Guinea, who learn a counting system based on _____ _____ _____ .

9. To learn and remember the long lists of names and facts encountered in school and at home, children need to master new _____ for storing and retrieving information.

10. Dr. Robert Siegler notes three ways children learn new cognitive skills. One is _____, where children see someone else perform a task and later repeat it themselves. A second method is through _____. Lastly, children often _____ new cognitive strategies, even if the old strategies still work.

11. Dr. Ellen Winner studies gifted children and has identified their three key characteristics as:
(a) _____; (b) _____; and
(c) _____ .

*Concrete operations*

12. When Mayan children first learn to weave, they need to prepare a complex winding board, even though the board does not bear a physical resemblance to the way the threads will look on the loom. This skill involves _____ _____ (seeing the correspondence mentally first), a hallmark of concrete operations.

13. Part of concrete operational thought is understanding that an object or thing can change while retaining its underlying _____, as is demonstrated in Piaget's conservation tasks.

*Moral development*

14. School-aged children can understand and appreciate what motivates someone else's actions, and this ability helps them develop their own set of _____ values.

15. Within mostly gender-segregated miniature cultures, boys and girls develop different _____ for governing social behavior.

*Aggression*

16. Male peer groups often engage in rough, verbally provocative behavior and sometimes show high levels of _____ aggression.

17. As Dr. Nicki Crick explains, girls are more likely to use _____ aggression. That is, they are more likely to use the relationship as a means to hurt someone's feelings when they feel hurt themselves.

18. A _____ is someone who teases or threatens beyond what the peer group finds acceptable.

*Friendship and helping others*

19. Peers help in the development of _____ behavior, offering aid without obvious benefit to you.

20. According to Dr. Nancy Eisenberg, _____ is when an individual feels the same emotion as another person, based on the person's cues or the situation they are in. When a person feels _____, however, they don't necessarily feel the same emotion as another person, but they do feel sorrow or concern.

21. According to Dr. Robert Selman, two functions of friendship are (a) to share _____ and (b) to develop one's _____, that is, to be able to assert one's own ideas and needs, and to work out differences with others.

*Thought questions*

22.   Identify all of the factors that are responsible for gender segregation.  Do not forget factors that may arise from children themselves.  Think about your own experiences in elementary school when answering this question.

23.  Do you think it is possible for parents to increase the chances that their son or daughter will be considered gifted in school?  Do you think parents *should* attempt to cultivate a gifted child?

24.  What can parents and teachers do to help children become more empathetic?

## B. OBSERVATION MODULE ASSIGNMENTS

1. Two schoolgirls talking about toys and boys (4:20)

a. Describe the context and content of this interview with two seven-year-old girls, Phyllis (on the left) and Kim.

b. Although these two girls don't say so directly, it's quite clear that they are friends. As you watch this video segment, what is it about their behavior and language that reflects the nature of their friendship?

c. Describe these girl's thoughts about boys and boyfriends. How much time do children of this age typically spend with peers of the opposite sex?

d. What questions would you ask these two girls if you wanted to probe their understanding of the nature of friendship?

2. An elementary school lesson on grammar (3:00)

a. Describe the context and content of this video segment.

b. Given the content of this lesson and the quality of these children's answers, what do you think is the average age of this group of students? Justify your estimate.

c. Listen to all of the answers of these students, and try to identify a child who seems to have the best grasp of this material. What assignment would you give this child to further his or her understanding of this material on sentence structures?

d. Observe how the teacher has organized this lesson and how she interacts with each member of the class. Describe briefly all the ways she is facilitating the growth of their understanding of grammatical rules.

3. Interviews with 9- and 10-year-olds at school (6:20)

a. Summarize the content of Brian's answer to the question, "Can you tell us a little bit about yourself, maybe about your family?" To what extent does Brian answer with psychological qualities to describe himself?

b. Summarize the content of Xavier's answer to the question "Tell us a little bit about yourself." Xavier says he doesn't have a best friend—yet. If you were this boy's parent or teacher, what kinds of things could you do to help him meet potential friends?

c. Summarize the content of Ashley's answer to the question, "Where are you from and what's your family like?" How would you describe her understanding of friendships and of herself?

## C. FIELD ASSIGNMENTS

1.  A time-sampling analysis of time spent with same-sex peers

Researchers of child development often want to know how an individual or a group of children distribute their time among various activities. A classic example is Mildred Parten's study of children's social participation in various play activities, such as solitary play, parallel play, and cooperative play. Parten's study suggested that children's play changes in a stage-like manner, where parallel play is an intermediate play between solitary activity and truly social-cooperative play. Later research modified this view by showing that parallel play is often used as a "lead-in" to cooperation among children (Bakeman & Gottman, 1997).

For this assignment you will be using a common method of observational research, time sampling, to assess the proportion of time children spend (a) alone, (b) with peers of the same sex, (c) with peers of the opposite sex, and (d) with peers of both sexes. Every 30 seconds you will code the child's behavior, until five minutes has elapsed. Then you will repeat this procedure until you have coded four children across 20 minutes.

Start by making a coding sheet like the one below, or you can photocopy this one. You will also need a stopwatch (or a wristwatch with a large face and clearly visible second hand). It is also recommended that you complete this assignment in pairs, where one person keeps time and the other observes.

A playground is an ideal place to observe, where you can see children of both genders in a variety of activities. Begin by selecting four children to observe; if possible, choose two boys and two girls. Write their names (or brief descriptions), sexes, and ages (or approximate ages) on the data sheet before you begin coding. You will observe each child for five consecutive minutes before switching to the next child. While observing the child, note if they are playing alone (A), playing with one or more boys (B), playing with one or more girls (G), or playing in a mixed group of male and female peers (M). After each 30-second interval, write the appropriate code to the right of the time. Note that in *interval coding*, the clock tells you when to code. If the child's behavior falls into more than one code category—say, Alex plays with a boy for a few seconds, and then jumps rope with a group of girls—choose the one code that best fits how he spend most of his time during the 30-second interval.

When you are finished coding four separate children, calculate the proportion of time each child spends with members of the same sex. For example, if Alex is coded "B" for a total of six intervals, the proportion of time he spends with same-sex peers is 60 percent. In class, you can compare your data for boys and girls with other students' data, to see if a consistent pattern emerges. Also, note if the tendency to play with children of the same sex is stronger for children ages 6 through 8 compared to children 9 through 11.

Time Sampling Procedure

Key to Codes:  A = alone / B = boy partner(s) / G = girl partner(s) / M = mixed partners

| Time | Code | Name | Sex | Age |
|------|------|------|-----|-----|
| 00:30 | _____ | _____ | _____ | _____ |
| 01:00 | _____ | | | |
| 01:30 | _____ | | | |
| 02:00 | _____ | | | |
| 02:30 | _____ | | | |
| 03:00 | _____ | | | |
| 03:30 | _____ | | | |
| 04:00 | _____ | | | |
| 04:30 | _____ | | | |
| 05:00 | _____ | | | |
| 05:30 | _____ | _____ | _____ | _____ |
| 06:00 | _____ | | | |
| 06:30 | _____ | | | |
| 07:00 | _____ | | | |
| 07:30 | _____ | | | |
| 08:00 | _____ | | | |
| 08:30 | _____ | | | |
| 09:00 | _____ | | | |
| 09:30 | _____ | | | |
| 10:00 | _____ | | | |
| 10:30 | _____ | _____ | _____ | _____ |
| 11:00 | _____ | | | |
| 11:30 | _____ | | | |
| 12:00 | _____ | | | |
| 12:30 | _____ | | | |
| 13:00 | _____ | | | |
| 13:30 | _____ | | | |
| 14:00 | _____ | | | |
| 14:30 | _____ | | | |
| 15:00 | _____ | | | |
| 15:30 | _____ | _____ | _____ | _____ |
| 16:00 | _____ | | | |
| 16:30 | _____ | | | |
| 17:00 | _____ | | | |
| 17:30 | _____ | | | |
| 18:00 | _____ | | | |
| 18:30 | _____ | | | |
| 19:00 | _____ | | | |
| 19:30 | _____ | | | |
| 20:00 | _____ | | | |

2. Rules for contact with the opposite sex

Throughout the world, middle childhood is a time where boys and girls choose to spend most, but not all, of their free time with peers of the same sex. Same-sex peer groups are important contexts for learning about the normative ways of thinking, talking, and acting. On the playgrounds of industrialized countries, boys are more likely to move around in larger groups, while girls are more likely to prefer smaller groups with closer friends. It is not unusual for specific same-sex groups of children to have explicit rules for when and when not to interact with children of the same sex. You can find out if children in your neighborhood have such rules by asking them.

For this assignment, interview one eight-year-old boy and one eight-year-old girl, on separate occasions, on the topic of "When is it OK to play with a girl (boy)?" Before you start, think of a few specific questions you can ask. For example:

- Is it OK for boys to play with girls? Why?
- Is it ever not OK for boys to play with girls? Why?
- Some kids say if a boy touches a girl he can get "cooties." What does it mean to get cooties?

If possible, tape record their responses, and write two brief summaries, one for boys and one for girls, of the rules for touching members of the opposite sex. When you are finished, note if either the boy or the girl seemed to have stronger views about interacting with children of the opposite sex. This will make a terrific classroom discussion topic if everyone interviews at least one child.

3. Conservation of liquid

School-aged children, compared to preschoolers, are much more logical and systematic in their problem-solving efforts and in their speech. A classic demonstration of logical thinking is Piaget's conservation of liquid task. After reading your text and watching the appropriate section of the video, try administering the conservation of liquid task to two children, one who is about five to seven years old, and a second who is about eight years of age or older. Tape record their responses and write a brief summary of (a) the procedure you followed, (b) the key answers they provided, and (c) your interpretation of their mental status with reference to concrete operational thought.

# Adolescence

## A. NARRATED VIDEO ASSIGNMENT

*Key terms*

conformity
ejaculation
formal operational thought
growth spurt
logical thought
menstrual period
puberty
sexual identity

*Physical development*

1. One of the first signs of puberty is a growth spurt, around age _____ for girls and about age _____ for boys.

2. During this growth spurt, the _____ lengthen before the upper body, yielding a gangly look for some adolescents.

3. Girls have a higher ratio of _____ to _____, and hence will look rounder and softer compared to boys.

4. Dr. Ann Peterson stated that there may be some negative consequences of late puberty for _____. In addition, there may be problems associated with early puberty for _____.

*Cognitive development*

5. Jean Piaget identified a new quality of thinking in adolescents that he called _____ _____ . Teenagers can think systematically about all logical relations within a problem.

6. Another quality of teenage thinking is their ability to consider _____ , and not just realities.

*Social and emotional development*

7. Younger adolescents refer to _____ events and people to discuss hypothetical questions about fairness or justice.

8. Older adolescents are more likely to refer to _____ _____ and will strive to consider alternative points of view.

9. The new psychological awareness that adolescence brings can lead to crippling _____ _____ .

10. While peer groups provide encouragement and guidance, teenagers feel less pressure to _____ after their fifteenth birthday.

*Thought questions*

11. What can parents do to help a teenage daughter who is experiencing distress because puberty occurred early?  Is there anything you think parents should avoid doing or saying in this circumstance?

12. What social and cognitive factors account for the differences between the quality of moral reasoning between younger and older adolescents?

13. Is there any particular teenager in this video that seemed most similar to you and your way of thinking about issues when you were their age?  Describe what this teenager said and the way their thoughts seemed similar to your own.

## B. OBSERVATION MODULE ASSIGNMENTS

1. Adolescent girl and boy talking about sexuality (7:45)

a. Listen to Trezure as she describes the consequences of early sexual maturation for girls. How would you summarize her thoughts on this topic?  How old would you judge Trezure to be?

b. What role can parents play in helping an adolescent girl deal with the physical and social changes of puberty, according to Trezure?

c. What are Stephen's thoughts on the consequences of early sexual maturation for boys?  How old would you judge Stephen to be?

d. What qualities does Stephen look for in a potential girlfriend?  How do Stephen's thoughts compare with the normative expectations of your peer group?

e. What qualities does Trezure look for in a potential boyfriend?  How do Trezure's thoughts compare with the normative expectations of your peer group?

2. Discussion of the play *A Streetcar Named Desire* (2:25)

a. Listen to this discussion of a character's motivations in the Tennessee Williams's play *A Streetcar Named Desire*. How would you describe some of the judgments expressed on the conduct of Blanche, a mature woman who had an affair with a 17-year-old student?

b. What reasons are given for their judgment of Blanche's behavior?

c. How do you think this discussion would be different if all of the students in this class were 13 years old?

3. Two adolescent boys talking about politics and dating (14:35)

a. Describe Terry's (age 16) and John's (age 13) attitudes toward immigration. What factors do they cite as responsible for their attitudes? Are there any other factors that they did not mention which may be important in shaping the political attitudes of adolescents?

b. According to Terry, parents have a greater influence on his behavior, but John says peers have a greater influence. Describe their thinking on this subject. Do their ages have anything to do with the differences in their opinions on the importance of parents in the lives of teenagers?

c. Describe Terry's attitudes about dating. Do his opinions on the subject seem typical for adolescent boys his age?

d. Describe John's attitudes about dating. If you met John and he asked you for advice on dating, what would you tell him?

## C. FIELD ASSIGNMENTS

1.  Resolving conflicts with parents

Adolescents often have definite ideas about how to get along with parents, and how to balance their needs for freedom and responsibility with their parents' needs and concerns for their well being. Conflict is inevitable at times, although most adolescents surveyed by psychologists report feeling close to and respectful of their parents. But exactly how do adolescents view conflicts with parents?

If you can find an adolescent boy or girl to speak with, ask them about any conflict that has happened in the past week or two with a parent. What started the conflict? What were their needs, and how did they perceive their parent's point of view? How was the conflict resolved?

When you are finished discussing this topic, ask him or her about the worst fight they ever had with a parent since becoming a teenager. Again, probe the inner and outer context of the situation, how they and their parent perceived the conflict, and how it was resolved.

If possible, tape record your conversation as an aid to memory, and write up your interview in a page or two. Be certain not to use the adolescent's real name in your write up, for privacy's sake.

2.  Adolescent risk taking

Adolescence is a time of new freedom and responsibility. And sometimes an individual or a group may decide to do something, like drink and drive, although at some level they know they are taking a risk that could have severe consequences. Why do adolescents take risks, and why is risk taking important, and even enjoyable, to adolescents?

Find an adolescent boy or girl, and ask them about the kinds of risks they or their friends take, and why. You must insure that their answers will be kept in confidence and that they do not have to tell you anything they are not comfortable speaking about.

Because of the potentially sensitive nature of this material, it may be best not to tape record your interview. But take good notes, write down some of their exact phrases, and try to get a sense of why risk taking is important—perhaps necessary. Write up your interview in a page—more if you need it—and be certain not to use the adolescent's real name or any other identifying information. (If you find this topic of interest, take a look at Cindy Lightfoot's 1997 book, *The Culture of Adolescent Risk Taking*.)

# Early Adulthood

## A. NARRATED VIDEO ASSIGNMENT

*Key terms*

antithesis
anorexia nervosa
body mass index
bulimia nervosa
cohabitation
collagen
dialectical thought
divorce rate
drug addiction
homeostasis
infertility
in vitro fertilization
organ reserve
postformal thought
senescence
set point
synthesis
social clock
thesis

*Physical development, senescence, and homeostasis*

1. Between our _____ and _____ birthdays, we're at the peak of our athletic capabilities.

2. The gradual decline of physical capacities is called _____ .

3. One of the first age-related changes of the body is the loss of _____, the connective tissue of the body, which leads to wrinkling of the skin.

4. With increasing age, it is more difficult for the body to maintain _____, its internal state of balance.

5. Another age-related change is a decrease in _____ _____, the extra capacity of the internal organs and muscles that the body uses to adjust to stress or extreme conditions.

*Health and dieting*

6. A preoccupation with weight and constant, aggressive dieting can lead to eating disorders such as _____ _____ and _____ _____.

*Fertility*

7. Almost 15 percent of couples experience _____, which is usually defined as the lack of a successful pregnancy after one year of regular intercourse without contraception.

8. _____ _____ _____ is a technique in which egg cells are fertilized with sperm in a laboratory.

*Cognitive development*

9. A more subjective, interpersonal, and flexible way of thinking, _____ _____, begins to dominate adult mental life. This style of thinking is less abstract and absolute than formal thought, and is often better suited to solving real-world problems.

10. Another sign of young adult cognition is _____ _____, the ability to consider opposing ideas and to forge them into a new belief. In this type of thinking, each idea (thesis) and its opposite (antithesis) continually evolve (synthesize) into deeper and more refined ideas.

*Cohabitation, marriage, and divorce*

11. The _____ _____ refers to the idea that each society has standards concerning the appropriate age for particular behaviors and accomplishments.

12. According to Dr. Ronald Sabatelli, couples that _____ are more likely to break up compared to legally married couples, in part because of the absence of a formal legal structure that surrounds the relationship.

13. The United States has one of the highest _____ rates in the world.

14. According to Dr. Sabatelli, homes experiencing marital distress are less likely to be _____ focused.

*Thought questions*

15. What factors do you think would reduce the risk of developing an eating disorder in young adulthood?

16. Describe an example of your own dialectical thinking, or that of someone you know.

17. According to your experience of the social clock, at what minimal age is it optimal for couples to cohabitate or marry? What reasons can you offer?

## B. OBSERVATION MODULE ASSIGNMENTS

1. Interview with a young man about work and friends after college (7:20)

a. Listen to Mannes as he describes thoughts and feelings about work. Can you tell what it is about work he doesn't like?

b. Mannes describes himself as "socially awkward." Listen carefully to what he says about interactions with coworkers, with strangers outside of work, and with friends. From what you read about earlier in this course, would you describe him as being temperamentally shy? Explain your reasoning.

c. Describe Mannes' reflections about work and friendships in relation to Erik Erikson's stages of psychosocial development.

d.  How old would you judge Mannes to be, and how long do you think it has been since he graduated from college?

2. A young man returns to college to prepare for medical school (5:30)

a. John explains that college is not as difficult this time around compared to his first experience, even though he is taking difficult premedical coursework.  What factors could explain the fact that he experiences college as easier and less stressful?

b.  Describe John's reflections about work and friendships in relation to Erik Erikson's stages of psychosocial development.  In what ways are John and Mannes different in their psychosocial identity?

c.  John made a decision to go back to college to pursue his former goal of becoming a doctor.  In what ways do you think his experience would be different if he chose to go back to college at age 30?

## C. FIELD ASSIGNMENTS

1.  Love and work in early adulthood

Sigmund Freud believed that "love and work" were the reasons for human existence. Most writers in the social sciences and humanities would agree at least in part with Freud's assessment: connecting with others, and doing things well, are powerful motives throughout the life span and in particular for young adults. The years after high school or college often bring the first "real" job and the first serious commitments.

Interview a young adult, age 22 through 30 and not currently in a serious committed relationship, about the characteristics they believe would be essential in a life partner or spouse. Ask this same person about the characteristics of work that are most important for their long-term happiness and fulfillment.

Tape record your interview, so later you can quote them or paraphrase accurately in your write-up. Ask open-ended questions, and see if you can get your interviewee to explain the reasons behind his or her preferences. After the interview, write a report in three parts: (a) A brief description of the person (first name only) and the setting for the interview; (b) two or more paragraphs describing his or her preferences for a partner and for a career; and (c) your reactions to his or her answers. You may also want to comment on the compatibility between his or her ideas about commitment and about work.

2.  Plotting the social clock

Each subculture has its own social clock, "a culturally set timetable that establishes when various events and endeavors in life are appropriate" (Berger, 2001, p. 513). In this assignment you will measure and plot the social clock of a specific cultural subgroup.

Photocopy or type the questionnaire below, and administer your survey to 10 young adults, all of the same gender and belonging to the same cultural subgroup (e.g., Mexican-American males, European-American females). Next, calculate the average and the range of values for each of the 6 social clock questions. Write up a brief report of your survey findings, first reporting the data (averages and ranges) in chronological order to show the time progression for these cultural expectations. Then write a paragraph or two discussing your findings.

## Social Clock Questionnaire

The social clock refers to the cultural norms about the "best" age for various social events and accomplishments, such as learning to drive, finishing school, starting a career, getting married, having a baby, etc.

For each of the statements below, fill in a *number* that represents the "best" age, according to *your specific cultural group*, for each of the events and accomplishments.

Note that you may have your own thoughts on what age would be best for you. Nonetheless, for this questionnaire you should fill in the ages that you understand to be "best" according to your specific cultural group.

YOUR BACKGROUND

1. What is your age? _____
2. Which cultural group best describes your ethnic background and gender?

_____ (e.g., Mexican-American male,
                                            African-American female,
                                            Anglo-American male, etc.)

SOCIAL CLOCK QUESTIONS

Fill in the best age, according to the norms of your culture/gender group, for each of the following:

1. _____ getting married
2. _____ becoming financially independent from parents
3. _____ learning to drive a car
4. _____ establishing a career
5. _____ finishing school
6. _____ having a first baby

# Middle Adulthood

## A. NARRATED VIDEO ASSIGNMENT

*Key terms*

arthritis
diabetes
gender convergence
hypertension
lupus
menopause
osteoporosis
plasticity
midlife crisis
role reversal
sandwich generation

*Health and nutrition*

1. At least two recommendations for good nutrition and health are consistently supported by research:
(a) avoid too much _____, and (b) get enough _____ in your diet.

2. Women who work out just 3 hours a week reduce their risk of heart attack by about _____.

3. People who are _____ and _____ tend to be healthier than people who live in rural areas, and have less money and education.

*Ethnicity and health*

4. African-Americans tend to be at greater risk for _____ and _____, and have lower rates of recovery from diseases such as breast cancer.

*Sex differences in health*

5. Women tend to live longer than men, in part because men _____, _____, and _____ more.

6. Women are at greater risk for chronic diseases such as _____, _____, and _____ .

*Menopause*

7. According to Dr. Michelle Warren, some of the common (but temporary) symptoms of menopause include _____, _____, and _____ .

*Brain development and learning*

8. According to Dr. Kurt Fischer, the brain is constantly _____ as a function of experience.

9. The brain is remarkable for its _____. We can learn new things well into old age.

*Personality*

10. Most people are more content in _____ adulthood than in any other period in their life span.

11. Few people experience the fabled midlife crisis. Our _____ don't change very much, so those of us who do experience a midlife crisis are the same people who experienced a crisis earlier in life.

*Gender convergence*

12. Most people in their 40s and 50s experience a loosening of traditional gender _____ .

*Relationships with children, parents, and partners*

13. According to Dr. Catherine Cooper, many people in middle adulthood may experience a role _____, as they take on more of the caregiving for their parents.

*Thought questions*

14. What factors might explain why the incidence of certain diseases, such as diabetes, varies across ethnic groups?

15. What kinds of activities can you imagine yourself doing if your goal was to stay cognitively flexible and alert well into old age?

16. What factors do you think best account for the widespread observation of gender convergence in middle adulthood?

## B. OBSERVATION MODULE ASSIGNMENT

1. A middle-aged man speaks about fishing and family (7:35)

a. How would you describe his psychosocial identity with reference to Erik Erikson's theory?

b. Did you note any evidence of gender convergence in this interview?

c. Describe his view of his personality development between young and middle adulthood.

d. From what you have heard in this interview, what style of parenting do you think he usually endorses in relating to his son?

2. Woman speaks about being single and older (10:25)

a. Describe Edie's thoughts on the problems men and women face in their 60s when seeking companions.

b.  What are some of the things Edie is doing to help meet a potential male companion?  Are there any behaviors or situations she wishes to avoid?

c.  What are some of the positive qualities of Edie that would be an asset to an intimate personal relationship?

d.  What specific manifestations of ageism" does Edie describe?  Are there any ways to avoid or reduce the consequences of ageism as you grow older?

## C. FIELD ASSIGNMENTS

1.  How people feel about what they do all day

In his book *Working*, Studs Terkel presents the stories of American working people in all walks of life—the wealthy, the poor, professionals, laborers, and housewives (Terkel, 1974). His book probes deep into the motivations, hopes, disappointments, and passions of his subjects. It's a great read, and I recommend you take a look at some of his interviews before you begin the current assignment.

Interview someone, aged 40 to 65, who has been in a particular career or specific work setting for at least 10 years. Sample questions are listed below:

- Why did you choose this line of work?
- When you first started, did you think you would be here as long as you have? Why?
- Are you passionate about this line of work? If not, is it something that pays the bills? Is it something in between?
- What kinds of skills—technical or interpersonal—does this line of work require?
- What are some of the important life lessons you have learned in this line of work?
- Do you experience conflicts between work and home life?  How have you balanced the two?

Tape record your interview, so you can capture the interviewee's exact sentiments.  Your write-up should have three parts: (a) Describe the person and the setting of the interview; (b) Describe the content of the questions and answers; and (c) Write a paragraph or two of commentary—your thoughts—on his or her description of work and its meaning.

## 2. Long-term relationships

Many of the students enrolled in a class on developmental psychology will know firsthand what it is like to live away from home, to work full time, and to be in a stable relationship. However, few will know from direct experience what it is like to be in an intimate relationship for over a decade. The point of this field assignment is to speak with and observe a couple who have been married for at least 10 years.

Find a couple married for 10 or more years and ask if each would agree to be interviewed at the same time. Ask each of them, in turn, how they met, what they liked about the other then, and what they like about the other now. Ask each of them how much time they now spend together, and which activities they do together and which apart. Then ask each what, if anything, they find annoying about the other person, and what, if anything, about themselves annoys their partner. Finally, ask them what they have learned in their time together about how to make a marriage work.

Before the interview, write out each of your questions, and leave space below for notes on their answers. But most important, take note of the answers as well as partner's nonverbal reactions. Does the wife ever roll her eyes or scrunch her face when the husband speaks? Does the husband smile or chuckle when his wife speaks? Tape record your interview, so you can preserve both the content and the nonverbal qualities of their responses. In your write-up of this interview, describe (a) the two interviewees and the setting of the interview; (b) the content of their answers as well as their nonverbal reactions to each other; and (c) your thoughts about the things they said and their nonverbal reactions to each other.

In preparation for this interview, you may want to take a look at John Gottman's book on marital interaction, *Why Marriages Succeed or Fail* (Gottman & Silver, 1995). His scientific research is based on direct observation, physiological measurement, and questionnaires of married couples over the past 20 years. Pay particular attention to his description of the nonverbal behaviors that predict which marriages will succeed and which have a high probability of ending in divorce.

# Late Adulthood

## A. NARRATED VIDEO ASSIGNMENT

*Key terms*

Alzheimers disease
assimilation
cataracts
dementia
demography
glaucoma
sensory register
working memory

*Demographics of aging*

1. According to Dr. Robert Butler, around _____ percent of the population will be over 65 shortly after the year 2000, and this percentage corresponds to _____ of the voting population.

*The senses*

2. Common eye diseases among older people include _____ and _____, and almost all older people need eyeglasses or contact lenses.

3. About one third of people in late adulthood suffer from _____ loss.

*Mobility*

4. A serious concern for some older people is loss of mobility, a common side effect of bone _____ and loss of muscle _____ .

*Information processing and memory*

5. As the _____ _____ declines, it takes longer to process and record information. _____ _____ also becomes less efficient.

6. Research has shown that _____ _____ can postpone memory loss by improving the flow of blood to the brain.

*Dementia*

7. _____ is the most damaging of the dementias, and is characterized by forgetfulness and an eventual inability to control basic life functions.

8. For some older adults, nursing homes are the best solution for the problem of providing 24-hour care. The best nursing homes cater to a person's _____, _____, and _____ needs, and allow them to make many of their own decisions.

*Social and emotional aspects of late adulthood*

9. It is not true that most people in late adulthood will suffer from _____ or show a lack of _____ activity.

10. Research has shown that very often the later years of long-term relationships are the _____.

11. An important part of our later years is _____ the past and sharing our memories with our loved ones.

*Thought questions*

12. In your opinion, what will be the political consequences of the increase in the proportion of retired persons in the early part of the 21st century?

13. If in your own middle adulthood your parents moved into the same house with you, how might that change your relationship with them?

14. If you could spend an entire afternoon with the oldest living member of your extended family (e.g., grandparent, great-grandparent, grandparent's sister), what kinds of questions would you like to ask them?

## B. OBSERVATION MODULE ASSIGNMENTS

1. An old woman talks about love and about death (7:20)

a. Describe Georgeanne's experiences as a young woman. How old would you estimate her age to have been at that time, and how old do you think she is now?

b. What are Georgeanne's beliefs about love and fidelity? Compare her attitudes on this subject to your own.

c. Describe Georgeanne's attitude about death. How does her view of death compare to your own?

d. If you could ask her one question about love, what would it be?

2. An old man, age 99, talks about life in a nursing home (7:10)

a. What was Bill's occupation before retirement?  How long did he work at this job, and when did he retire?

b. What advice does Bill give for staying healthy in old age?

c. Bill has experienced some hearing loss in his later years.  Does this seem to bother him much?

d. What methods does he use to compensate for problems of remembering other people's names?

e. If you could ask this man one question about his experience of the 20th century, what would it be?

## C. FIELD ASSIGNMENTS

1. Photography and memory

We are accustomed to thinking of memory as something inside of us—something we have.  Psychologists, however, regard memory as process—something we do.  We perform a mental search when we try to recall the name of a childhood friend, but we can also do a physical search through our diaries and through albums of photographs.  The focus of this assignment is to look closely at how older individuals use photographs to record and recall the past.

Visit the home of an older relative or neighbor—someone who is over 65 years of age—and ask them if they will show you photographs of their childhood and early adulthood, of their own parents, and every-day scenes of life whey they were growing up.  If they agree, see if they mind if you tape record your conversation with them.  This way, you can concentrate on what they have to say.

Ask any questions about the past you feel comfortable asking.  I've done this several times with my grand-mothers, and I'm always eager to know what day-to-day life in the city was like.  For example, where did they shop for meats and vegetables? What street vendors came down the block every week? Where would kids play after school and in the summer?

For your write-up, describe (a) the person and the setting, (b) the content of their descriptions of the past, (c) how photographs were used to remember the past, and (d) your reactions to their memories.  Pay atten-tion to where photographs are kept in the house, and how often they seem to refer to photographs in order to remember and share the past.

2. Life's lessons

The point of this field assignment is simple:  What advice will people in late adulthood offer to the next generations?  Ask at least two relatives over the age of 65—man and woman, if possible—what advice they would offer to a person at the start of adulthood.  The advice can be specific (e.g., about marriage or work) or it can be general (e.g., about core values).  Write up this assignment and include (a) a brief description of the persons interviewed and the setting, (b) the content of their advice, and (c) your thoughts on the advice given.

# Further Readings and Other Resources

Bakeman, R., & Gottman, J. M. (1997*). Observing interaction: An introduction to sequential analysis.* Cambridge, UK: Cambridge University Press. (Originally published 1986.)

Although its primary goal is to introduce techniques for analyzing sequences of behavior observations, Bakeman and Gottman's brief text provides a concise and non-technical discussion of behavior-coding systems in the first three chapters. Chapter 4 provides a clear explanation of inter-observer reliability and its measurement (e.g., Cohen's Kappa).

Cartwright, C. A., & Cartwright, G. P. (1974). *Developing observation skills.* New York: McGraw-Hill.

Intended primarily for teachers and students of education, this brief text introduces a few specific techniques for observing and recording behavior in the classroom (e.g., tallying behavior frequencies, behavior checklists and rating scales, and anecdotal records).

Irwin, D. M., & Bushnell, M. M. (1980). *Observational strategies for child study.* New York: Holt, Rinehart and Winston.

Irwin and Bushnell's handbook provides an excellent overview of the history of various observational strategies, including the recording of narratives (e.g., diary descriptions, anecdotal records, running records, specimen descriptions, case studies, and field studies), time sampling, event sampling, checklists, and ratings systems. Each chapter is followed by lab assignments on observation.

Slee, P. T. (1987). *Child observation skills.* London: Croom Helm.

Slee's brief yet informative text describes a variety of observation techniques used in the study of children within the traditions of psychology, sociology, anthropology, and education. Chapter 4 contains practical exercises to illustrate various methods of observation (e.g., diary descriptions, anecdotal records, specimen descriptions, event sampling, time sampling, rating scales). More so than other books on direct observation, this text discusses the value of qualitative and interpretive (i.e., hermeneutic) approaches to observing and understanding human behavior. Also, methods of assessing children in school contexts are reviewed. A particularly useful appendix contains summaries of six observation schemes used in contemporary research and references to the original journal articles where they are described.

Whiting, J. W. M., Child, I. L., & Lambert, W. W. (1966). *Field guide for a study of socialization.* New York: John Wiley and Sons.

This field guild—a manual for anthropologists conducting field research—provides a fascinating view of the process of collecting detailed information for a major cross-cultural analysis of socialization. While intended for advanced field researchers, it contains suggestions of value to anyone interested in recording child and adult behavior in natural contexts. Chapters include specific examples of interview questions, categories of behavior to observe, and rating systems.

# References

Bakeman, R., & Gottman, J. M. (1997*). Observing interaction: An introduction to sequential analysis.* Cambridge, UK: Cambridge University Press. (Originally published 1986.)

Brownell, W. C. (1879). The art schools of Philadelphia. *Scribners Monthly*, 18 (September), 745.

Cole, M., & Cole, S. R. (1996). *The development of children* (3$^{rd}$ ed.). New York: W. H. Freeman.

Doyle, A. C. (1975). *The complete adventures and memoirs of Sherlock Holmes.* New York: Bramhall House. (Original stories published in *Strand Magazine* 1891-1893.)

Gottman, J. M., & Silver, N. (1995). *Why marriages succeed or fail: And how you can make yours last.* New York: Simon & Schuster.

Lightfoot, C. (1997). *The culture of adolescent risk taking.* New York: The Guilford Press.

Strayer, F. F. (1991). The development of agonistic and affiliative structures in preschool play groups. In J. Silverberg & P. Gray (eds.), *To fight or not to fight: Violence and peacefulness in humans and other primates.* Oxford: Oxford University Press.

Turkel, S. (1974). *Working: People talk about what they do all day and how they feel about what they do.* New York: Pantheon.

Valsiner, J. (1988). *Child development within culturally structured environments, Vol. 2: Social co-construction and environmental guidance in development.* Norwood, NJ: Ablex.